Iraq

by Miriam Aronin

Consultant: Marjorie Faulstich Orellana, PhD
Professor of Urban Schooling
University of California, Los Angeles

BEARPORT
PUBLISHING

New York, New York

Credits

Cover, © Rasoul Ali/Dreamstime and © asiseeit/iStock; TOC, © Heritage Image Partnership Ltd/Alamy; 4, © ton koene/Alamy; 5L, © DEA/C SAPPA/AGE Fotostock; 5R, © Bilal Izaddin/Shutterstock; 7, © Bilal Izaddin/Shutterstock; 8L, © douglas knight/Shutterstock; 8R, © yeowatzup/CC BY 4.0; 9, © Michael Runkel/imageBROKER/Alamy; 10–11, © Images & Stories/Alamy; 11R, © Eric Lafforgue/AGE Fotostock; 12, © Images & Stories/Alamy; 13, © Michael Runkel/imageBROKER/Alamy; 14, © keithwheat/iStock; 15, © Caroline Penn/Alamy; 16–17, © rasoul ali/Alamy; 17R, © dpa picture alliance/Alamy; 18, © Fedor Selivanov/Shutterstock; 19, © Kamira/Shutterstock; 20, © Trinity Mirror/Mirrorpix/Alamy; 21, © Stocktrek Images, Inc./Alamy; 22, © Johnny Saunderson/Alamy; 23, © Images & Stories/Alamy; 24L, © Michael Runkel/Alamy; 24–25, © Zoonar/URS FLUEELER/AGE Fotostock; 26T, © Ton Koene/AGE Fotostock; 26B, © Foodio/Shutterstock; 27, © Nadir Keklik/Shutterstock; 28, © mooinblack/Shutterstock; 29, © Aflo Co. Ltd./Alamy; 30T, © Olegmit/Dreamstime and © Asafta/Dreamstime; 30B, © Gerry McCann/ZUMAPRESS/Newscom; 31 (T to B), © rasoulali/Shutterstock, © Angela Ostafichuk/Shutterstock, © padchas/Shutterstock, and © AGF Srl/Alamy; 32, © Lefteris Papulakis/Shutterstock.

Publisher: Kenn Goin
Senior Editor: Joyce Tavolacci
Creative Director: Spencer Brinker
Design: Debrah Kaiser
Photo Researcher: Thomas Persano

Library of Congress Cataloging-in-Publication Data

Names: Aronin, Miriam, author.
Title: Iraq / by Miriam Aronin.
Description: New York : Bearport Publishing, 2018. | Series: Countries we come from | Includes bibliographical references and index.
Identifiers: LCCN 2017039238 (print) | LCCN 2017040291 (ebook) | ISBN 9781684025343 (ebook) | ISBN 9781684024766 (library)
Subjects: LCSH: Iraq—Juvenile literature.
Classification: LCC DS70.62 (ebook) | LCC DS70.62 .A76 2018 (print) | DDC 956.7—dc23
LC record available at https://lccn.loc.gov/2017039238

For more information, write to Bearport Publishing Company, Inc., 45 West 21st Street, Suite 3B, New York, New York 10010. Printed in the United States of America.

10 9 8 7 6 5 4 3 2 1

Contents

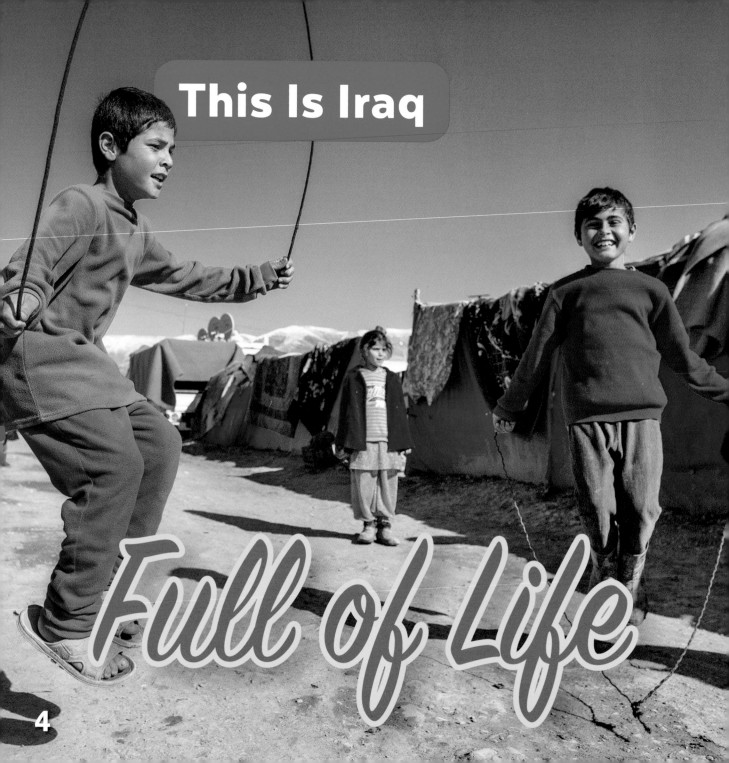

This Is Iraq

Full of Life

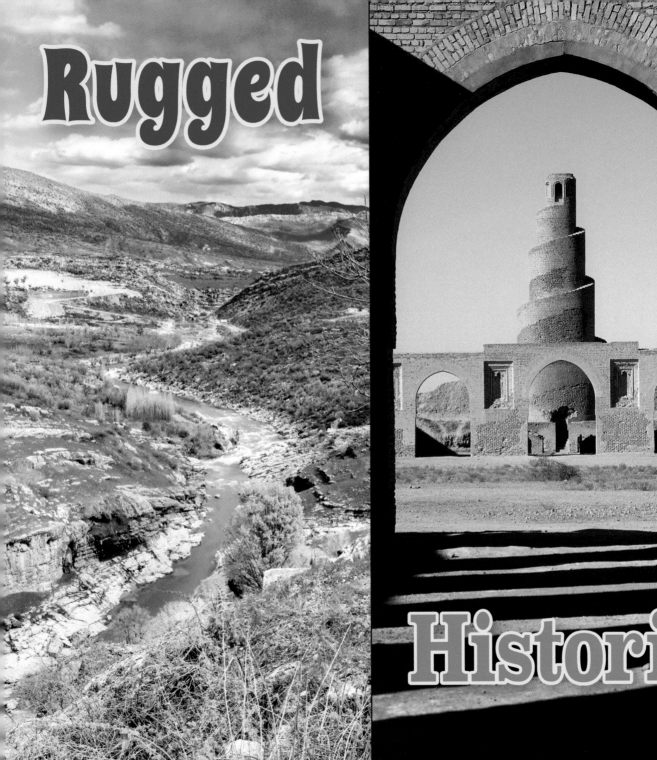

Rugged

Historic

5

Iraq is a country in the Middle East.
More than 39 million people live
in Iraq.

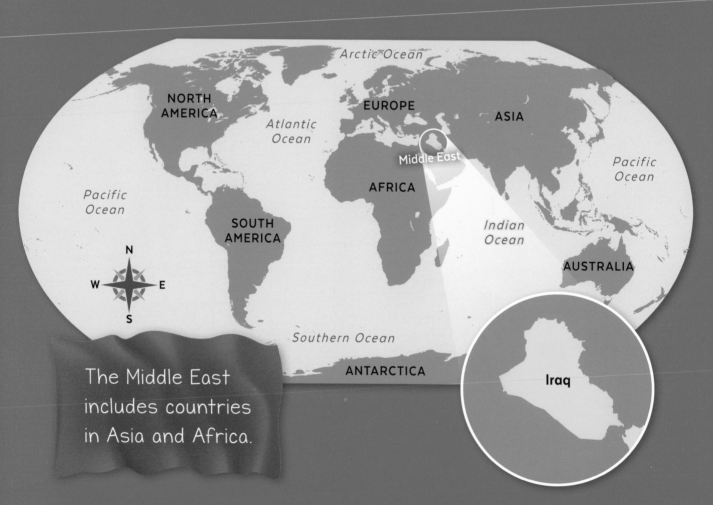

The Middle East
includes countries
in Asia and Africa.

Arctic Ocean

NORTH
AMERICA

Atlantic
Ocean

EUROPE

ASIA

Middle East

Pacific
Ocean

AFRICA

Pacific
Ocean

Indian
Ocean

SOUTH
AMERICA

N

W   E

S

AUSTRALIA

Southern Ocean

ANTARCTICA

Iraq

a cafe in Iraq

7

Iraq has different kinds of land.
There are rocky deserts.

oil pump

A lot of oil lies under Iraq's land. The oil is used to make fuel and other products.

The country also has steep, snowy mountains.

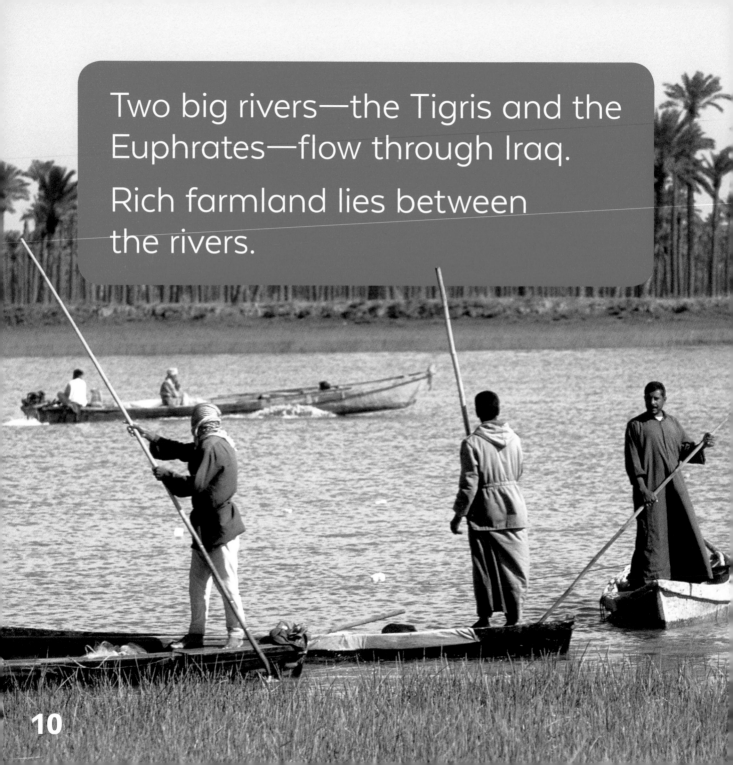

Two big rivers—the Tigris and the Euphrates—flow through Iraq. Rich farmland lies between the rivers.

Iraq was once called Mesopotamia. This word means "land between the rivers."

Most Iraqis live in this area.

They grow crops and raise animals.

The people of Iraq are **diverse**.

Arabs make up the biggest group.

Other groups include Kurds and Turkmen.

Kurdish people live in northern Iraq.

Iraq has two main languages—
Arabic and Kurdish.

This is how you say *market* in Arabic:

Suq (SOOK)

This is how you say the same word
in Kurdish:

Bazar (BAH-zar)

More than
24 different
languages are
spoken in Iraq.

Arabic writing

14

Iraqi market

15

The **capital** of Iraq is Baghdad.
It's also the country's biggest city.

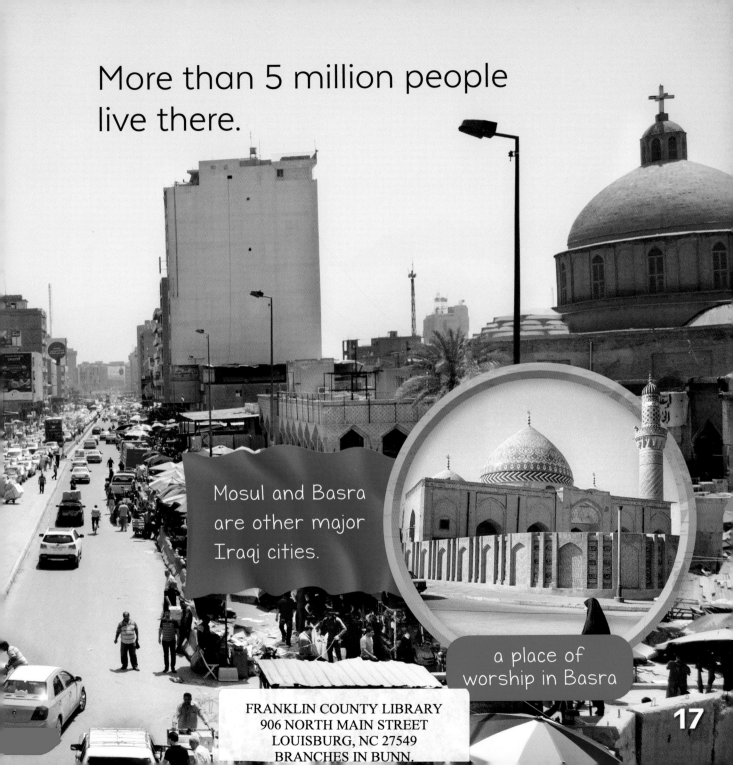

More than 5 million people live there.

Mosul and Basra are other major Iraqi cities.

a place of worship in Basra

17

Iraq has a long history.

The Sumerians lived there about 5,000 years ago.

Sumerian stone carving

They created the world's first written language.

It's called cuneiform (kyoo-NEE-uh-form).

The Sumerians wrote on clay, not paper.

In **modern** times, Iraq has seen many wars.

From 1979 to 2003, a harsh ruler, or dictator, controlled Iraq.

He hurt thousands of people.

The United States helped remove the dictator from power in 2003.

a statue of the ruler being taken down

Today, the Iraqi people rule themselves.

Iraqi soldiers

21

Religion is important to the Iraqi people. Most Iraqis are Muslim.

Muslims worship at **mosques**.

Muslims pray five times each day.

Family is the center of Iraqi life.

Grandparents, parents, and children often share the same home.

a Kurdish grandmother

Many Iraqis belong to large family groups called tribes. A tribe can include more than 10,000 people!

Meals in Iraq start with snacks called *mezza*.

Then people eat a main dish with rice.

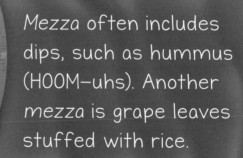

Mezza often includes dips, such as hummus (HOOM–uhs). Another *mezza* is grape leaves stuffed with rice.

Iraqis enjoy grilled meat, fried chickpea balls, and fish.

Many Iraqis love soccer.

Iraq's soccer team is known as the Lions of Mesopotamia.

Crowds gather to watch games.
The sport brings people together!

Fast Facts

Capital city: Baghdad

Population of Iraq:
More than 39 million

Main languages:
Arabic and Kurdish

Money: Iraqi dinar
(DEE-nar)

Major religion: Islam

Neighboring countries include:
Syria, Saudi Arabia, and Iran

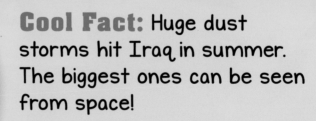

Cool Fact: Huge dust storms hit Iraq in summer. The biggest ones can be seen from space!

capital (KAP-uh-tuhl) a city where a country's government is based

diverse (dih-VURSS) varied

modern (MOD-urn) having to do with the present

mosques (MOSKS) buildings used by Muslims for worship

31

Index

Read More

Murray, Julie. *Iraq (Explore the Countries).* Minneapolis, MN: Abdo (2016).

Owings, Lisa. *Iraq (Exploring Countries).* Minnetonka, MN: Bellwether (2016).

Learn More Online

To learn more about Iraq, visit
www.bearportpublishing.com/CountriesWeComeFrom

About the Author

Miriam Aronin lives in Chicago, Illinois. She loves learning about countries and cultures around the world.